# I AM

# EXISTENCE

## Oluwafemi Oluwadurotimi Popoola

**OLUWAFEMI OLUWADUROTIMI POPOOLA**

ISBN: 979-8-8370-5121-0

Unless otherwise indicated, all Scripture quotations are taken from the King James Version of the Bible.

I AM EXISTENCE

I AM
EXISTENCE

# Dedication

"God is good all the time; He's got the whole world in His Hands." How come then there is so much evil in the world? Does God not have control over evil?

Maybe the concepts of sin and evil that we've been taught all along have missed some critical piece of understanding. What this book attempts to offer is another perspective on good and evil; light and darkness; sin and the holiness of God.

If any of these questions has plagued you or even just casually crossed your mind, this book is dedicated to your hunger and thirst for truth.

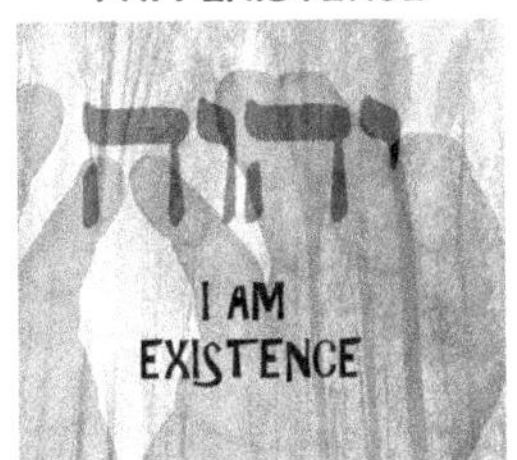


# Contents

# Introduction

In all the years that I have had a concept of good and evil; which goes back to the earliest days when my parents would scold or discipline me for something I did "wrong", I had come to accept that the great conflict of the universe is the war between good and evil. I accepted the idea that there is a good God and an evil devil and both are in conflict with each other over the fate of the universe.

When I came into the knowledge of Jesus Christ and came under the teachings of different saints and pastors and started reading the Bible for myself, I came to the understanding (at that time) that in the conflict between good and evil, good wins.

From the Christian perspective it is believed that Jesus Christ (the Messiah) is the embodiment of good and Satan (the devil) is the embodiment of evil. We read in the scriptures; particularly in the gospels, how Jesus Christ was crucified and resurrected and through this secured the victory of good over evil for all eternity.

This book offers a slightly different perspective. *It is the intention of the author to provide a broader understanding of God and His position, Satan and his position and man's position in the order of existence. This book also offers an alternate perspective on common concepts like sin, evil and the nature of the warfare we as Christians are called to.*

Throughout the Old Testament, our God is called by His personal Name YHVH written in the King James Version of the Bible as the LORD. Repeatedly, especially in the books of Exodus and Leviticus where God Almighty reveals Himself to the Israelites, He makes the statement "I AM YHVH" (I Am the LORD). One quick thing to point out in this is that God Almighty wants to be identified by His Name. Imagine how rude it would sound if you walked into the office of a person of great importance and referred to them the entire time as "Man" or "Woman". That's exactly how it is when we relate to The Almighty God and only call Him 'God'.

I always wondered what the Bible meant in 1 Samuel 17 when it said that Goliath cursed David by his gods and David responded "I come to thee in the name of the LORD", until I was watching a movie once and a character in the movie bellowed out in exasperation "In the name of Odin…" and I almost fell out of my chair. It suddenly hit me that none of those guys ever went around saying "God bless you" or "God will do it" or "God is able" as we do today. They ALWAYS mentioned the specific name of the specific god they were referring to or they would bless a person by invoking "the gods" (elohim) when they were not sure which of the gods the person they were blessing preferred.

In the land of Egypt, there were many gods according to their culture and traditions. They included Osiris, Set, Amun, Anubis, Thoth, Isis, Sekhmet, just to name a few. Each of these entities had its own particular traits, habits, likes and dislikes and specific actions they required from devotees as a form of worship. The concept of one Almighty God as the default god that everyone acknowledged as God did not exist, so people always mentioned the name of the specific god they had in mind.

The Israelites also all did it; and they had to in order to identify WHO they were talking about. They had spent all those many years in Egypt with myriad gods whose presence and power they were very familiar with and some of them had come to trust in. When YHVH brought them out through Moses, the people of YHVH had to always proclaim the Name of YHVH so as not to mask the worship of another deity under so generic a term as "god".

The Name YHVH in itself is quite revealing and we will see just by examining the meaning of that name how the God of the Hebrews stands apart from all other gods (elohim) that scriptures and contemporary knowledge have identified.

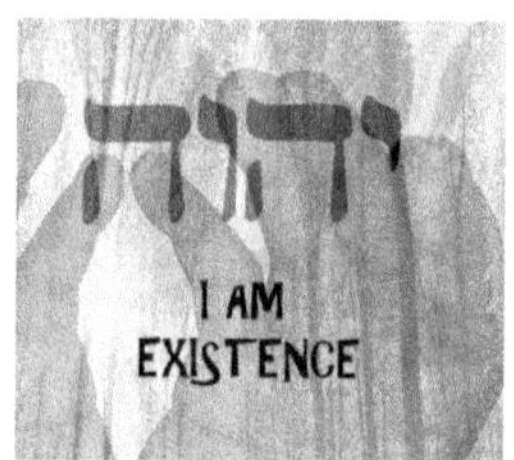


**Thou hast created *all things* for Thy pleasure!**

**Rev 4:11**

# 1

# In The Beginning... Elohim

Before YHVH created anything, there was only YHVH. There are several truths in this statement that may fly in the face of what is generally accepted about the God of the Bible.

First controversial concept; YHVH is not one person.

Many Christians accept the concept of the Father, Son and Holy Spirit in a theoretical/theological sense, but in reality believe that the God they worship is one person with three different offices or responsibilities. This idea (amongst many others) of explaining the concept of the Trinity is a result of centuries of the mantra insisting that Judaism, Christianity and Islam are the three monotheistic religions of the world. This has further allowed a belief to form; that the singular god worshipped in each of these three religions is actually the same entity who is just worshipped in different forms.

The very word Elohim which is translated as God in the first sentence of the entire scriptures is a plural word. The Trinity is not a theological concept of one person who manifests in three different forms; it is literally three People who make up a council that is better referred to as "the Godhead". There are three personalities that make up the Godhead of Israel with the unique peculiarity of being in perfect unity amongst themselves; unlike the pantheons of other polytheistic beliefs who are always quarrelling, fighting and being jealous of one another.

In Deuteronomy 6:4, the verse that is often misquoted and misinterpreted to account for the Christian and Jewish monotheistic belief, Moses says, "Hear, o Israel: The LORD our God is one LORD". When we condense this statement about the God of the Hebrews, it literally says:

Hear, o Israel: YHVH our elohim (plural) is one YHVH

The key word in this statement; "One" as with most other Hebrew words has several uses which include but are not limited to the following:

One = First.

This can be translated into suggesting that Moses was telling the children of Israel that the God they worship should be put first in all matters pertaining to their daily living. It also suggests that the God they worship is the first amongst other gods and should be given the highest reverence. Should the Israelites presume that it's okay to revere other gods so long as they revere YHVH above the others, He ensures that they understand that this is not acceptable by making it the very first of the Ten Commandments which are the very foundation of the Hebrew faith.

One = United.

This can be translated into suggesting that Moses was telling the children of Israel that the Personages that make up the Godhead called YHVH are completely united in purpose. To approach one is to approach all three and the people need not look for ways to appease one against another or play one off the other as could be done with other pantheons of gods in other cultures. In other cultures it was not uncommon for adherents of the same broad religion to have a favorite god which they gave their adoration to in order to manifest the peculiar trait of that god. YHVH is not so. This Elohim is to be given reverence as one body much as one would give reverence to a panel of judges deciding one's fate in unison.

In Genesis 2, when YHVH would make man, One of the personalities called for a conference on how man would be formed and what would be the nature of this creature they were about to form when He made the statement "Let Us make man…"

In Genesis 11, when men were building a tower up into Heaven contrary to what YHVH would permit; one of the personalities spoke to the others and said, "Let us go down and confound their language…"

If the God of the Bible was one entity operating in three different 'offices' as some of us have been taught, when referring to Himself, He would not use the word "We" or "Us" or in any way refer to Himself in the plural form.

One question to consider is; if the Godhead was in the beginning, where did they exist? Another question would be; how long had they existed?

Our concepts of time and space are entirely based on geographical location to which YHVH is not limited as YHVH fills eternity. YHVH is existence and outside of YHVH nothing exists. Everything YHVH created was not created outside of YHVH but within the bond that binds the three Personalities that make up the Godhead. It was within the framework of this bond that Heaven and earth were created. The name of the bond is a word we throw around a lot and often misinterpret on purpose or by accident: LOVE.

The three Personalities of Elohim, bound to one another with the bond of Love, made the decision to bring into existence other entities that would now be *created* by Love and within the framework of Love.

The primary emotion that the reality of Love produces is ecstasy. Job 38:6 and 7 says that when YHVH laid the foundations of the earth, the sons of Elohim shouted for joy. Usually the phrase "sons of Elohim" refers to the angels; so the angels experienced ecstatic joy as they watched YHVH create other things after creating them.

In the book of Revelations, whenever John saw visions of Heaven, there was usually great joy amongst the inhabitants. All the horrors described in that book relate to occurrences on the earth. In Heaven; the realm where YHVH's desire is accomplished, there is unspeakable joy, unspeakable peace and wellbeing. Psalm 16:11 says that in YHVH's Presence is fullness of joy and at YHVH's right hand, there are pleasures forever more.

*"Fullness of joy" and "pleasures forevermore" are what YHVH intends for all creation and it was with this intention, in this context and in this environment that all creation was created.*

In Genesis 1, after YHVH created Heaven and Earth, YHVH began to move things around; and each time YHVH did, YHVH said that it was good. Even a casual observation of the things YHVH created, separated or manifested in Genesis 1 reveals things that are necessary to sustain life.

There is one peculiar truth tucked away in this story of creation that we would do well to investigate; the unraveling of which mystery will give us a more robust understanding of the Awesomeness of YHVH, the futility of the devil's scheming and the great delusion and misfortune of the humans he has enlisted through empty promises.

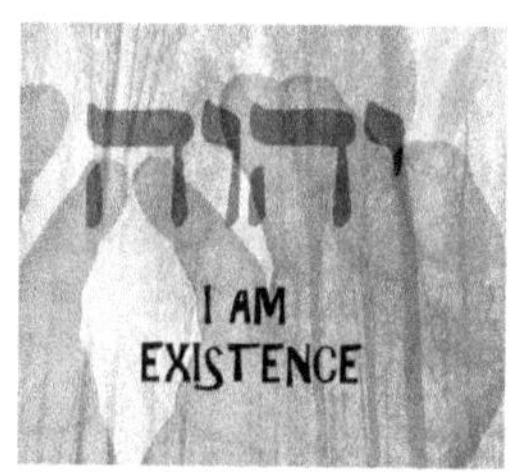


I make peace, and create evil: I the LORD do all

these

Isaiah 45:7

# 2

# What is Evil?

The first time we come across the existence of a concept of evil is in Genesis 2. YHVH told Adam that he must not eat from the fruit of a tree called the Tree of the knowledge of good and evil. As Adam went about his duties as the keeper of the garden in Eden that YHVH had created, a creature which the Bible identifies as the most "subtle" (not evil) of all the creatures that YHVH had created, came to the female (Adam)[1]. By a mighty sleight of hand, he got the female to eat of the tree and then the male: and

---

[1] Genesis 5:2 tells us that YHVH created the male and female and called them Adam. The male Adam looked at the female Adam when she was presented to him and called her "Woman". In Genesis 3:20, the male Adam further complicates things by changing the name of the female once again to "Eve"

through this act, there was a seismic shift in the order of YHVH's creation:

- The male and female Adam were kicked out of the garden

- They were both denied access to the Tree of Life

- They were both aware of things they should not have been aware of/were not intended to be aware of according to the design of their Maker (i.e. their nakedness)

- The male and female became separated in identity when the male changed the name of the female from Adam to Eve.

Note that the serpent didn't offer the female one of its eggs or its venom or even the scales on its skin to consume; the entity that contained the evil which

Adam was forbidden to eat from, was wholly separate from the being of the serpent. The serpent did not make them imbibe its nature to partake of "good and evil", it only pointed them in the direction of how to access it.

The point of all this is simply that evil does not originate with the serpent (satan). Evil is a reality that exists apart from the devil/satan. So where then did evil come from? The Bible states it plainly; but for most of us, our prior stamped-in-concrete classification of good God and evil satan won't let us accept it.

Isaiah 45:7 I form the light, and create darkness: I make peace, and create evil: I the LORD do all these *things.*

*Evil is a realm of YHVH's reality which the nature and framework of man as designed by*

*YHVH is not suitable to carry, occupy, experience or operate in.*

When the Israelites went out to war and brought back spoils of war in Numbers 31:23, Moses instructed the warriors to purify all the spoils they were bringing in by two elements: Water and fire. The nature of some of the items was such that they had to be purified only with water. If they had been passed through the fire, the fire would have destroyed them (clothes, goat's hair, wood), but other things were to be purified with fire (gold, silver, precious metals).

Numbers 31:19-23  And do ye abide without the camp seven days: whosoever hath killed any person, and whosoever hath touched any slain, purify *both* yourselves and your captives on the third day, and on the seventh day.  And purify all *your* raiment, and all that is made of skins, and all work of goats' *hair,* and all things made of wood.  And Eleazar the priest said unto the men of war which went to the battle, This *is* the ordinance of the law which the LORD commanded Moses; Only the gold, and the silver, the brass, the iron, the tin, and the lead; Everything that may abide the fire, ye shall make *it* go through the fire, and it shall be clean: nevertheless it shall be purified with the water of separation: and all that abideth not the fire ye shall make go through the water.

The tree of knowledge of good and evil was a doorway to a realm of reality that the frame work YHVH created mankind for was not meant to experience; just as cloth is not meant to experience fire.

Satan did not lie when he said that eating from the tree would make the woman like gods to know good and evil; what he conveniently forgot to mention was that gods are capable of knowing that realm of existence without being corrupted or damaged by it but the frame work of man is not.

A quick example of this is where YHVH says "Vengeance is mine; I will repay." Nobody metes out vengeance on another by sending them flowers. Vengeance is exacted upon a person by bringing an evil upon them for some injustice they have exacted upon another. YHVH says: "I AM capable of exacting vengeance and when I do, it will be righteous, because only I have the capacity to mete out vengeance without becoming corrupted." When a man metes out vengeance, the framework of man is not designed to carry that reality and so the man becomes corrupted and his actions become the doorway for evil into his own life.

There is a curious case of vengeance/justice mentioned in 1 Kings. YHVH gave a Word of prophecy to Jeroboam because he (Jeroboam) who YHVH had anointed to replace the lineage of David, had himself committed a great sin in leading the nation into idolatry.

1 Kings 14:7-11  Go, tell Jeroboam, Thus saith the LORD God of Israel, Forasmuch as I exalted thee from among the people, and made thee prince over my people Israel,  And rent the kingdom away from the house of David, and gave it thee: and *yet* thou hast not been as my servant David, who kept my commandments, and who followed me with all his heart, to do *that* only *which was* right in mine eyes; But hast done evil above all that were before thee: for thou hast gone and made thee other gods, and molten images, to provoke me to anger, and hast cast me behind thy back: Therefore, behold, I will bring evil upon the house of Jeroboam, and will cut off from Jeroboam him that pisseth against the wall, *and* him that is shut up and left in Israel, and will take away the remnant of the house of Jeroboam, as a man taketh away dung, till it be all gone. Him that dieth of Jeroboam in the city shall the dogs eat; and him that dieth in the field shall the fowls of the air eat: for the LORD hath spoken *it.*

A few years later, Jeroboam died and his son Nadab began to rule; as is the manner of kings. At this point, a man called Baasha took upon himself to fulfill the Word of prophecy spoken by Ahijah the prophet over Jeroboam. The Bible actually says that what Baasha did was a fulfillment of that prophecy; to mete out vengeance upon the enemy of YHVH whose actions had led Israel into transgression. This was an error they would not repent from until they were captured centuries later and taken into Assyria; and then to the ends of the earth.

1 Kings 15:25-31 And Nadab the son of Jeroboam began to reign over Israel in the second year of Asa king of Judah, and reigned over Israel two years. And he did evil in the sight of the LORD, and walked in the way of his father, and in his sin wherewith he made Israel to sin. And Baasha the son of Ahijah, of the house of Issachar, conspired against him; and Baasha smote him at Gibbethon, which *belonged* to the Philistines; for Nadab and all Israel laid siege to Gibbethon. Even in the third year of Asa king of Judah did Baasha slay him, and reigned in his stead. And it came to pass, when he reigned, *that* he smote all the house of Jeroboam; he left not to Jeroboam any that breathed, until he had

destroyed him, according unto the saying of the LORD, which he spake by his servant Ahijah the Shilonite: *Because of the sins of Jeroboam which he sinned, and which he made Israel sin, by his provocation wherewith he provoked the LORD God of Israel to anger.* Now the rest of the acts of Nadab, and all that he did, *are* they not written in the book of the chronicles of the kings of Israel?

Unfortunately for Baasha, he also did not walk in the ways of YHVH and he continued to lead Israel into error (as mentioned earlier, the transgression of the 2 calves Jeroboam erected to be worshipped went on uninterrupted for centuries until they were captured by the king of Assyria and the land of Samaria was repopulated with heathens). However when YHVH pronounced judgment on Baasha to bring evil upon him, there was an interesting reason YHVH gave besides the fact that Baasha provoked YHVH to anger by practicing idolatry.

1 Kings 16:7 And also by the hand of the prophet Jehu the son of Hanani came the word of the LORD against Baasha, and against his house, even for all the evil that he did in the sight of the LORD, in provoking him to anger with the work of his hands, in being like the house of Jeroboam; *and because he killed him.*

## Marriage

Another example of this concept of good and evil that may make it clearer is marriage. In Genesis 1, YHVH worked through the six days of creating the earth and the inhabitants. Over and over YHVH declared that what was done was good. There was clearly a certain kind of idea YHVH had of what YHVH wanted the earth to be like; which was wholly different from what Heaven was like. Consequently, the inhabitants YHVH created to occupy Heaven would operate under different rules and guidelines from the inhabitants of Earth.

The one time YHVH looked upon the work and saw something that did not fit the environment YHVH had made on earth was when YHVH noticed that man was alone in his species. YHVH considered it necessary to create a female version out from inside the man in a move to better the lot of Adam with regards to his environment.

It is instructive to know that man is the only creature whose female version was created in this fashion. Every animal YHVH created had the male and female created simultaneously and separately out of the dust of the ground. YHVH chose to build the female human out from inside the male. This is the basis for union; what we call marriage, and YHVH is the One Who is able to identify who on earth has been formed from the rib of whom and thus bring them together. It is why animals don't get married, they just mate. They don't need union or oneness, they just need to multiply. From animals we can see that sex is not the key to oneness or union; there is a platform that must first exist for sex to complete it the way YHVH intended. If that platform does not exist, then what is established is not union/oneness but bondage.

Back to the concept of marriage as it relates to good and evil. YHVH said "It is not good" which in essence means, it doesn't fit this environment to have this situation; or in other words, it is evil… for man to be alone. YHVH then moved to correct the situation and the female was formed; fully with the intention of being the sexual partner of the male, and YHVH rejoiced in the idea of the male and female engaging themselves in sexual activity within the framework of their oneness.

Jesus said in Matthew 22:30 that when humans resurrect, they will be as angels in Heaven which neither marry nor are given in marriage. The environment YHVH created in Heaven is one that does not require its occupants to engage in marriage and sexual activity. The same way YHVH said "It is not good for man to be alone" with regards to having a partner in covenant that the male relates to in all things including sexual activity, is the same way YHVH could say "It is not good for the angels to engage themselves in marriage and sexual activity." This statement is not entirely speculative because not long after Adam opened the doorway for evil into the human experience, angels from Heaven came down and "...took them wives of all which they chose" Genesis 6:2. This event of angels coming down and engaging in marriages resulted in entities being born on the earth that YHVH never intended. The presence and actions of these offspring of angels eventually led YHVH to destroying all land dwelling creatures through a great flood that spared only eight humans.

In summary, the concept of "evil" is not something that is against YHVH. It is an act or concept that is contrary to what YHVH has designed in a specific environment, for a specific place and for a specific type of His creation.

- Fire is not evil, but fire is evil if one attempts to use it to purify fabric.
- Marriage is not evil, but marriage is evil if Heavenly beings engage in it
- Sex is not evil, but sex is evil if it is not engaged in proper context (between a man and woman inside a covenant of marriage)

The tree of the knowledge of good and evil opened up humanity to *the ability* to learn things that are contrary to YHVH's order of events and activities designated for the environment called Earth.

# I AM EXISTENCE

Now then it is no more I that do it, but sin that dwelleth in me.

Romans 7:17

# 3

# What is Sin?

As crazy as this may sound, sin did not come into the world through Adam and Eve. Evil was introduced into the human experience when they ate the fruit; the nature of humanity was literally altered (imagine introducing fire to fabric) but sin came a little later.

Before we go into the concept of sin, we will take a little detour and discuss a very famous character amongst those who delve into the study of ancient and comparative religions, a character who the Bible mentions almost just as a side comment but whose life and activities have shaped history in unimaginable ways.

**Who is Nimrod?**

**Nimrod was first mentioned in Genesis 10 and the Bible seems almost reluctant to mention his name.**

Gen 10:8-14 And Cush begat Nimrod: he began to be a mighty one in the earth. He was a mighty hunter before the LORD: wherefore it is said, Even as Nimrod the mighty hunter before the LORD. And the beginning of his kingdom was Babel, and Erech, and Accad, and Calneh, in the land of Shinar. Out of that land went forth Asshur, and builded Nineveh, and the city Rehoboth, and Calah, And Resen between Nineveh and Calah: the same *is* a great city. And Mizraim begat Ludim, and Anamim, and Lehabim, and Naphtuhim, And Pathrusim, and Casluhim, (out of whom came Philistim,) and Caphtorim.

The descendants of Cush had been earlier introduced leaving Nimrod unmentioned, only for him to be mentioned by himself a little further on. Nimrod is credited with commissioning the building of the tower of Babel of Genesis 11. Babel is Babylon and the principles and practices Nimrod put in place have followed through the ages, right up to this time. The Book of Revelation tells us that Babylon will still be around and a great force of influence even at the tribulation of the end times.

Nimrod is recognized as the first king of the world and the first antichrist figure who some researchers have postulated will also be the last. I would like to propose a theory however that points to another key character mentioned in Genesis: the first murderer, Cain.

Genesis 4 tells us the well-known story of Cain and Abel. Two brothers brought their sacrifices to YHVH; the younger brother's offering was accepted but the elder's was not. Big brother got mad and killed baby brother and lied to YHVH about it while asking the cynical question "Am I my brother's keeper?" YHVH banished him and put a mark on him and then he all but fell off the face of the earth.

Some schools of thought have attempted to boost Cain's relevance in historical matters by suggesting that the statement in Genesis 6 referring to the sons of God mating with the daughters of men is actually talking about the good sons of Seth mating with the evil daughters of Cain. I will say no more about this theory.

What can be defended easily is that Cain's descendants till the sixth generation are mentioned in the Bible and we can be sure the Bible doesn't give us any irrelevant information. I recently noticed some interesting things about this character called Cain that I believe have had significant impacts on history.

*Cain let sin into the world.*

This may sound like an unscriptural statement but it was a statement YHVH literally made as plain as can be. After Cain's rejection, YHVH noticed that he was dejected and issued a warning to him which he failed to heed.

Genesis 4:6-8  And the LORD said unto Cain, Why art thou wroth? and why is thy countenance fallen? If thou doest well, shalt thou not be accepted? and if thou doest not well, sin lieth at the door. And unto thee *shall be* his desire, and thou shalt rule over him. And Cain talked with Abel his brother: and it came to pass, when they were in the field, that Cain rose up against Abel his brother, and slew him.

My understanding of this statement is that Cain was brooding over his lot and some thoughts were beginning to flash in his mind but had not taken root yet. The insidious spirits that flood the minds of men with diabolical thoughts and then teach them how to turn those thoughts into actions had not yet made this common practice. The idyllic background of Eden and the innocence that had been a precursor to these events had made such thoughts extremely difficult to form in the human mind. These feelings of rejection Cain was nursing were gradually opening up his mind to accept and act upon the thoughts that had hitherto been totally incompatible with human nature.

YHVH told him that if he continued to entertain those thoughts he would let sin in, and through this power of sin, he would rule. After he was banished from Eden[2] for his crime, he went east and built a city and called it Enoch after the name of his son (Genesis 4:16). Many researchers have done studies and mapped out Eden to cover the geographical areas extending from Egypt clear across to parts of Syria,

---

[2] Adam and Eve were banished from the garden but they were not banished from Eden. The garden was located inside Eden; it was not all of Eden.

Jordan and Saudi Arabia. East of this would place us somewhere in Iraq, the modern country in which the ancient city of Babylon is located. It is possible that the city Cain built and called after his son was simply rebuilt after the flood by Nimrod and called Babylon.

Genesis 4 tells us the sad story of Cain's rejection by YHVH, his bitterness towards his brother that led to murder and his playing smarty-pants with YHVH. After that, Cain's story is mostly ignored but the Bible proceeds to give us his genealogy and mentions some interesting things:

*There were 2 Enochs*

Enoch the 7th from Adam; the man who "walked with God: and he was not; for God took him" (Genesis 5:24) is very well known. He was from the line of Seth, the son God gave Adam and Eve after Abel was murdered and Cain was banished. He is part of the genealogy of ALL humanity today through the survival of the flood by Noah and his sons. He did some writing and his words are collected in a book which is referenced several times by the writers of scripture.

The other Enoch is 3rd from Adam, the son of Cain, a co-vagabond with his father; and I believe the person actually responsible for many mysteries that mystics erroneously ascribe to Enoch the 7th (descendant of Seth).

YHVH told Cain that if he gave in to what he was thinking, he would open a door for sin to come in and empower him to rule. He went ahead and did what he wanted and I believe this opened him up to strong spiritual persuasion and possibly habitation from entities that had long been looking for an opportunity to express themselves through humans.

It appears that Cain's descendants had an uncanny ability to be first in respective fields that play important roles in the world even today.

Enoch, the 3rd from Adam:

He is mentioned in the Bible as having a city built in his name. Now the Bible says that Cain actually built the city but he named it after his son Enoch.

There is a teaching amongst the schools of mystery that references a character called Hermes. Hermes is another name for Enoch and is often described as the 7th from Adam who walked with God and learned many mysteries; but I believe this a confusion of the 7th from Adam (son of Seth) and the 3rd from Adam (son of Cain)

Some of the things ascribed to Enoch as being first were:

- The science of city building: The Bible tells us that Cain built the first city recorded in human history and called it Enoch. If stories were passed down through word of mouth about a city called Enoch, it is likely that after one or two retellings the building of the city will be credited to the person it is named after.

- Hermes (Enoch the 3$^{rd}$ from Adam) is also credited with introducing writing to the world.

- Hermes (Enoch the 3$^{rd}$ from Adam) is also credited with introducing astronomy (the ability to read the heavenly bodies) and astrology (the ability to divine through reading the heavenly bodies) to the world.

Lamech, the 7th from Adam:

After Enoch, there were a couple of folk with no particularly interesting things mentioned about them; and then there was Lamech. Interestingly, just as nothing worthy of note seemed to be happening with Seth's descendants until the 7th generation when Enoch (the 7th from Adam) was born (and "walked with YHVH; and he was not: for YHVH took him", then he left a bunch of prophecies in his wake which writers of the New Testament quote freely), so also nothing interesting seemed to be happening with the descendants of Cain (except for the building of the first ever city on earth, east of Eden, likely in a place which I suspect eventually was rebuilt and called Babel), until Lamech (the 7th from Adam). He was born and grew up to become the first recorded polygamist. Polygamy doesn't seem like such a big deal today because of the many cultures that practice it, (even now some churches seem to wink at the practice) but it was a COMPLETE departure from YHVH's design for the family and must have taken a supernatural influence to birth the idea and carry it out.

Jabal, the 8th from Adam; Lamech's son:
He was the first recorded domesticator of cattle and first tent dweller. Abel was a keeper of sheep and this simply refers to his responsibility to care for them. Jubal however did not just keep cattle, but claimed *ownership* of them.

Jubal, the 8th from Adam; Jabal's brother:
He was the first composer of music.

Tubalcain, the 8th from Adam; Jubal and Jabal's brother
He was the first metal worker. No doubt his metal work was used in crafting tools for different purposes;

domestic as well as military. He would likely have crafted the first mattock and sickle for harvesting crops as well as the first sword and spears for harvesting people.

The essence of this genealogical investigation is to show how the descendants of Cain had advanced knowledge of things that would give them an edge over the rest of humanity in areas of culture and warfare. As YHVH said to Cain when he considered his line of action against his brother; "sin is at the door. If you let *him* in *he* will take you over and you will rule through *him*."

*This statement infers that sin is a personality or a class of personalities that cause the effects of the actions that we commonly call sin. In light of this understanding, sin is not the action but the personality inspiring that action.*

And again the anger of the LORD was kindled against Israel, and he moved David against them to say, Go, number Israel and Judah.

II Samuel 24:1

And Satan stood up against Israel, and provoked David to number Israel.

I Chronicles 21:1

# 4

# The Custodian

Before YHVH created anything, YHVH existed. Everything YHVH created took on a certain characteristic of YHVH as its primary expression. If you will, everything YHVH created; from the dust to the clouds to celestial bodies is a reflection of a characteristic of YHVH.

When YHVH made creation, YHVH handed over stewardship to a specific creation called Adam. The authority YHVH handed over to Adam only extended over the realm called Earth and did not extend into the realms called 'Heavens'.

In the different realms and sub-realms of the Heavens, authority was given to different creatures, some of whom we commonly refer to as angels. It is YHVH's desire to grant authority over sections of YHVH's creation to some of YHVH's other appointed creations.

We read of Joshua's encounter with a 'man' as Israel was preparing to take over Jericho. The 'man' presented himself as _Captain_ of the host of the LORD (Joshua 5:14).

In Daniel's encounter with the angel after his 21 day fast, the angel informed Daniel that he was only able to escape the blockade of the _Prince_ (ruler) of Persia after Michael; the _Prince_ (ruler) of YHVH's people came to his assistance (Daniel 10:13).

In the earthly realm, it's more clearly seen in the way YHVH appointed kings over YHVH's people; how YHVH appointed priests over YHVH's people, and how YHVH appointed prophets amongst YHVH's people.

Each of these offices typically did not cross over into one another's responsibilities. When King Uzzah entered the temple to offer incense, which was a strictly priestly responsibility, he was struck with leprosy. Even Moses, after he had anointed his brother as high priest, could not arbitrarily take on Aaron's responsibility for the simple fact that *responsibility is a function of authority and authority is a function of appointment.*

Ezekiel 28 is an extremely revealing section of the scripture with regards to one of YHVH's custodians. Referred to as the king of Tyrus, we are informed that he was a beautiful creature, an anointed cherub "for I have set (appointed) thee so."

Ezekiel 28:15-19 Thou *wast* perfect in thy ways from the day that thou wast created, till iniquity was found in thee.

By the multitude of thy merchandise they have filled the midst of thee with violence, and thou hast sinned: therefore I will cast thee as profane out of the mountain of God: and I will destroy thee, O covering cherub, from the midst of the stones of fire.

Thine heart was lifted up because of thy beauty, thou hast corrupted thy wisdom by reason of thy brightness: I will cast thee to the ground, I will lay thee before kings, that they may behold thee.

Thou hast defiled thy sanctuaries by the multitude of thine iniquities, by the iniquity of thy traffick; therefore will I bring forth a fire from the midst of thee, it shall devour thee, and I will bring thee to ashes upon the earth in the sight of all them that behold thee.

All they that know thee among the people shall be astonished at thee: thou shalt be a terror, and never *shalt* thou *be* any more.

This creature, who when we take holistically in the full context of the Bible, we identify as Lucifer and eventually Satan, was the custodian of YHVH's Light. He was the anointed cherub that covered or fenced off all other creation from direct contact with YHVH. Lucifer was literally the only creature that had direct access to the light of YHVH.

When iniquity was found in him, he was still the highest ranking creature and had to have authority over an aspect of YHVH's creation, so YHVH appointed him the custodian of darkness.

I have for a long time held to the notion that YHVH is Light so darkness cannot be a part of YHVH. I even went so far as to imagine that darkness is the absence of YHVH (because YHVH is Light). The truth is that everything that exists is an expression of YHVH;

*Darkness is an expression of YHVH's displeasure.*

YHVH's primary disposition is for Light, harmony, joy and pleasure. Psalm 16:11 says; "In Thy Presence is fullness of joy…" Revelations 4:11 says; "Thou art worthy o Lord, to receive glory honor and power: for Thou hast created all things and for thy Pleasure they are and were created."

YHVH created all things for His Pleasure, but that does not mean He cannot be displeased;

2 Samuel 11:27 And when the mourning was past, David sent and fetched her to his house, and she became his wife, and bare him a son. But the thing that David had done displeased the LORD.

Up until the time that iniquity was found in Lucifer, there was nothing to displease YHVH in all His creation; because He made everything for His

Pleasure. Within that framework, He appointed custodians over different aspects of the expression of that Pleasure. There was no expression of YHVH's displeasure and no reason for it, hence there was no creature appointed as a custodian over YHVH's displeasure.

When Lucifer sinned, he became it. Thus Lucifer fell from being the primary custodian of YHVH's Glory, the creature who fenced off all other creation from direct contact with the Glory of YHVH, to becoming the creature who was to mete out YHVH's displeasure on any other of YHVH's creation that would thenceforth displease Him.

*Thus Lucifer (the light bearer or prince of light) became Satan (the darkness bearer or prince of darkness).*

This fall would be comparable to being demoted by the board of a very large company from the position of CEO to the position of the toilet cleaner (specifically the toilets). It's easy to imagine that such a demotion wouldn't sit well with anyone and they would just submit their resume to another company. In this case though, there is no other company; everything that was created and any authority/position granted to any creature anywhere is created and granted by THE BOARD (Trinity). Lucifer, now Satan had to swallow the 'humble pie' and assume his new position with all the vitriol his bowels could muster. The only thing he could do however was to mess up the toilet so badly and keep it messed up so that would-be users would be turned off by the repulsiveness of the place. I think we can end this analogy here.

61

Now there was a day when the sons of God came to present themselves before the LORD, and Satan came also among them.

Job 1:6

# 5

# God Versus Satan?

The idea that "good is light - and evil is darkness" combined with the erroneous mantra that has confused many people in the church that "God is good all the time" (the Bible never says this), has given many people the notion that there is a cosmic struggle between good and evil and by extension between God and Satan.

*There is no struggle between light and darkness. What's more, light and darkness are not intrinsically opposed to one another; they are not mutually exclusive.*

In Genesis 1:4, YHVH saw that the light YHVH commanded into the earth (notice this was not the first introduction of light into *creation*, it was the introduction of light into the earth that was covered in darkness) was good, and YHVH divided/separated the light from the darkness (for purposes specific to the earth). Before YHVH separated the light from the darkness, light and darkness were occurring simultaneously.

Genesis 1:4 And God saw the light, that *it was* good: and God <u>divided</u> the light from the darkness.

It was only after YHVH separated the light from darkness (for purposes specific to earth), that light and darkness became "incompatible". In the full scope of reality, darkness is a reality that serves YHVH's purpose just as light is. YHVH seems however to prefer ALL creation to experience light rather than darkness.

For both light and darkness, YHVH has appointed custodians to administer the components of these realities upon creation; Satan (Lucifer) who used to be the custodian of Light, became the custodian of darkness due to YHVH's reassignment.

After Lucifer's attempted mutiny in Heaven (Isaiah 14:13-15), he was cast down to earth. As the newly appointed custodian of darkness, his new realm adopted his new nature/assignment and became covered in darkness as Genesis 1 tells us. He probably didn't appreciate his new position as the custodian of darkness, having been the custodian of light who walked in the Glory of YHVH and was the envy of all creation. But he adjusted nicely; he covered the entire realm of earth with his new nature. If he couldn't enjoy the light of Heaven, he could rule in the darkness of earth.

One day, he's picking his nose on a rocking chair in his front porch (or something) when he suddenly feels a weight, not just on himself but on everything. It's not an oppressive weight but he realizes what the Weight means: YHVH is moving/brooding and will likely soon make a decree that will change this new territory he (satan) was just starting to get comfortable in:

First, YHVH had stripped him of his power and position over all of YHVH's creation. At that time, there was no place to keep trouble makers; so YHVH sent him to earth and confined him there. He then thought he would have full sway over the earth (it's not the best of accommodations considering where he was coming from  but at least he had full sway over what goes on in this realm. He had changed the nature of the entire planet to suit his new nature, but now the

Spirit of YHVH had come and invaded his space again?! What did He want? What exactly was the game plan?

The answer to his haunting questions came in the statement made by YHVH; "Let there be light!" By this time it was obvious that YHVH was not going to turn an entire planet in his creation into a pit of darkness. In the 6 day creation, YHVH reconstructed the earth to suit the purpose He had intended for all His creation to be "good, good and very good". As a final blow to the devil, YHVH made a creature on the 6th day called Adam and gave Adam the stewardship over the earth. "Just because you're now the custodian of darkness does not mean you will have an entire planet to express that darkness over. In fact any administration of your darkness will have to be carried out under the supervision of this creature that was made from far inferior materials to those you were made from, but he will have my Spirit in him."

Satan wasn't going to have that so he devised a way to legally usurp the authority that YHVH had given Adam and once again have full sway over the earth. He however could not physically cover the earth in total darkness because the power to rule the light in the day had been given to the sun by YHVH, and even the night had a provider of light (the moon) that was outside of Adam's authority and hence outside of Satan's power to control after he stole that authority (Thank God!!!).

*In all of his raging against the plans of YHVH for the earth, for creation as a whole, for the individual destinies of YHVH's appointed creatures and for dominion on the earth, Satan is still just a custodian of YHVH's displeasure (darkness). What he does is try to influence people to do things to displease YHVH so he can be in the position to legally exert his authority over them.*

If a person does not and has not displeased YHVH in any way, Satan cannot have any rights to exert his authority over that person; because he is merely the custodian of YHVH's displeasure. He is like a corrupt police officer who dreams up ways to entrap people, so he sneaks around while law abiding people are sleeping and busts their brake lights, changes the tabs on their license plates to expired ones and other such traps so that when the person gets up in the morning and goes out they are in violation of the law and he can legally stop and harass them.

Proverbs 26:2 As the bird by wandering, as the swallow by flying, so the curse causeless shall not come.

John 14:30 Hereafter I will not talk much with you: for the prince of this world cometh, and hath nothing in me.

Without anything to accuse YHVH's creation of, Satan cannot implement his desire to mete out YHVH's displeasure upon creation.

*YHVH is not at war with Satan.*

Satan is merely an employee of YHVH, who is constantly trying to exert his influence over the rest of YHVH's creation even when he shouldn't.

*Light is not at war with darkness.*

*The only war really going on is the war each individual creature is in to keep Satan from "planting" something on them that would displease YHVH.*

This statement may sound overly simplistic, but it is the foundational war upon which every other battle is based; sorcery, divination, societal moral decay (which is really the aggregate of the moral decay of a critical mass of individuals).

In Numbers 22 and 23, we read how Balak, the king of Moab was afraid of being annihilated by these Israelites who's God had destroyed Egypt, and he called for Balaam to plant something upon the nation (a curse) that would cause YHVH's displeasure to be upon the nation so that they could get hammered. When YHVH refused to allow Balaam to curse the nation, he advised Balak to send in 'pretty little things' to entice the Israelite men; and it worked!

The very next chapter we read how Midianite women infiltrated the camp and led the men into fornication and idolatry. That was all Satan needed; YHVH's displeasure was upon the nation because of their transgression and he (satan) could now swoop down into action as the administrator of that displeasure; disease broke out in the camp and killed a bunch of folk.

The key thing to notice in all this is that Satan has no capacity to fight with YHVH; he can only wage war against YHVH's creatures. Even in this venture, his effort is totally fruitless if YHVH's creatures have not done or allowed anything that would cause YHVH's displeasure to be turned towards them.

Proverbs 26:2 As the bird by wandering, as the swallow by flying, so the curse causeless shall not come.

Satan is mad at YHVH. He's bitter, offended and incensed against YHVH, but can never be at war (in the true sense of the word) with YHVH. He is simply a custodian of YHVH's displeasure against YHVH's creatures, and can only get at YHVH by causing YHVH'S creatures to displease Him.

And being in an agony he prayed more earnestly: and his sweat was as it were great drops of blood falling down to the ground.
Luke 22:44

# 6

# Who is Victorious?

When Adam handed over the authority YHVH had given unto him to the devil, the devil had in a sense snatched something from the realm of YHVH's pleasure and trapped it in a state of YHVH's displeasure. Not that he (Satan) had taken it out of YHVH's Hands, he had just moved it (legally) from where YHVH wanted it to where He didn't want it. A not so great analogy of this would be for a steward in a large mansion to grab all the sterling silverware from the kitchen and use them as garden tools. It's still the same mansion, still the same Landlord and owner of the house, the kitchen, the garden and the gardener. The gardener just found a way to convert the use of it from fine dining and adornment to crude labor in the dirt of the garden.

When The LORD Yahshua came in the form of a baby, His assignment was to in a sense, reverse the use of as many of the silverware back to their original purpose. To do this, He had to overcome the temptation to allow anything Satan brought His way to convert His utility from a Vessel unto honor to a crude instrument. This is what the temptations in the wilderness were all about, and what the temptation in the garden was all about.

*The war that Yahshua had to win was the same war that every other one of YHVH's creation has to win; to avoid doing or receiving something that would cause YHVH's displeasure to come upon them.*

When Yahshua became a man, He was particularly vulnerable to this, even though He was fully YHVH.

Have you ever gotten mad at someone in traffic for doing something and found yourself doing the exact same thing to someone else; maybe even in the same trip/journey? It's always tough being on the receiving end of bad behavior. As the Divine Being, Yahshua, is utterly repulsed by certain human actions; but as a man, He was not immune to the tendencies to carry out those actions. He had to resist the temptations even unto blood.

Hebrews 12:4  Ye have not yet resisted unto blood, striving against sin.

In the garden of Gethsemane, Yahshua had to resist with all His might, the temptation to despise the Will of His Divine nature which is in line with the Will of the Father YHVH and the Spirit YHVH and choose the will of His own human nature. This would have been the first time that one Persona of the Trinity would have been contrary to the Others, and would have negated the Word spoken by Moses:

Deuteronomy 6:4  Hear, O Israel: The LORD our God *is* one LORD:

Any being, natural or divine that acts contrary to the Word/Law of YHVH has aligned itself with YHVH's displeasure and brought itself under the authority of the custodian of His displeasure; Satan. Just as Yahshua had to overcome the temptation to act contrary to the Word of YHVH, so every being created by YHVH has to overcome that inherent tendency, which was birthed when Adam first acted contrary to YHVH's instructions; and birthed that tendency in all of YHVH's creation on earth (not in Heaven).

79

And there was war in heaven: Michael and his angels fought against the dragon; and the dragon fought and his angels, And prevailed not; neither was their place found any more in heaven.

Rev 12:7-8

# 7

# The War in Heaven

Revelations 12:7-8  And there was war in heaven: Michael and his angels fought against the dragon; and the dragon fought and his angels, And prevailed not; neither was their place found any more in heaven.

This scripture is often debated on as to whether it speaks of a future war or if it refers to a war that supposedly happened when Satan first rebelled against YHVH. There is a lot of speculation; but the bottom line is that there was a war.

What was the nature of the war? What was at stake?

When we think of a war, we typically consider the wars we are familiar with: two parties are relatively equally matched and the dice can roll in any direction. Either party can outwit or outsmart the other and take possession of their enemy's property as spoil, then enslave or kill the soldiers and officers of their army.

Sometimes we think, when we read the Bible; that the army of light has an advantage over the army of darkness because Satan was only able to hoodwink 1/3 of the hosts of Heaven into his diabolical, doomed-to-defeat plan.

*The strength of the hosts of Heaven is not in their numbers but in the Pleasure/Purpose of YHVH.*

YHVH has committed more of His resources (Strength, Power, Will etc.) to His Pleasure than to His displeasure.

Nehemiah 9:17  And refused to obey, neither were mindful of thy wonders that thou didst among them; but hardened their necks, and in their rebellion appointed a captain to return to their bondage: but thou *art* a God ready to pardon, gracious and merciful, slow to anger, and of great kindness, and forsookest them not.

Psalms 103:8  The LORD *is* merciful and gracious, slow to anger, and plenteous in mercy.

Psalms 145:8  The LORD *is* gracious, and full of compassion; slow to anger, and of great mercy.

Nahum 1:3  The LORD *is* slow to anger, and great in power, and will not at all acquit *the wicked:* the LORD hath his way in the whirlwind and in the storm, and the clouds *are* the dust of his feet.

**The LORD is slow to anger, and thus would be less willing to release resources to execute His displeasure. Imagine if you will, a king who has several sports teams in his kingdom (jousting if you will), and one of the teams is his preferred team. The team members eat**

at the king's table, they get all the funding they need for better armor, and have access to the best trainers in the kingdom. The other teams have to come and make petitions to the king before he releases the resources for their most basic needs. These teams would have to have a lot of grit and willpower to even come close to competing with the favorite team.

This is for a situation where the king only supplies funds and physical resources. Now consider where the King supplies every resource including strength, wisdom, insight, counsel, superior resources (swords of fire as an example) and literally *everything* that would give His favorite team the advantage. Someone may consider that such a situation would not be fair and "God is a fair god." If you are laden with the idea that God is fair, the god you have in mind is not YHVH. YHVH is biased in favor of His Pleasure.

Psalms 16:11 Thou wilt shew me the path of life: in thy presence *is* fulness of joy; at thy right hand *there are* pleasures for evermore.


## YHVH keeps His Joy in His Presence and puts His displeasure far away from Himself.


Exodus 20:5 Thou shalt not bow down thyself to them, nor serve them: for I the LORD thy God am a jealous God, visiting the iniquity of the fathers upon the children unto the third and fourth generation of them that hate me;

Exodus 34:7 Keeping mercy for thousands, forgiving iniquity and transgression and sin, and that will by no means clear the guilty; visiting the iniquity of the fathers upon the children, and upon the children's children, unto the third and to the fourth generation.

Numbers 14:18 The LORD is longsuffering, and of great mercy, forgiving iniquity and transgression, and by no means clearing the guilty, visiting the iniquity of the fathers upon the children unto the third and fourth generation.

Deuteronomy 5:9 Thou shalt not bow down thyself unto them, nor serve them: for I the LORD thy God am a jealous God, visiting the iniquity of the fathers upon the children unto the third and fourth generation of them that hate me,

YHVH will only allow His displeasure to run its course through four generations. I believe it only lasts as long as that because the enormity of His Being will not allow one lifetime to contain the magnitude of His displeasure which according to Him, He doles out in trickles.

Deuteronomy 7:9  Know therefore that the LORD thy God, he *is* God, the faithful God, which keepeth covenant and mercy with them that love him and keep his commandments to a thousand generations;

1 Chronicles 16:15  Be ye mindful always of his covenant; the word *which* he commanded to a thousand generations;

Psalms 105:8  He hath remembered his covenant for ever, the word *which* he commanded to a thousand generations.

When it comes to YHVH's Pleasure however, YHVH hands it out in handfuls, and considering the size of YHVH's Hands, YHVH's pleasure cannot be contained in anything less than one thousand generations.

We who are made in YHVH's image can see a similar situation in our existence. When a person spends most of his/her time depressed, sad or angry, it begins to have adverse effects even on our physical bodies (not even considering all the spiritual and intellectual damage it will have done); a joyful attitude however has been proven scientifically to add years to our lives.

YHVH – the Godhead, Who is the Source of all things, all beings; living and non-living, Who by the Spirit sustain the very existence of all creation, is not embarrassed to affirm Their preference for Light over darkness, peace over chaos, joy over sorrow, righteousness over iniquity. YHVH has declared Their willingness to endow the custodians of light and YHVH's Pleasure with superior resources to the custodians of darkness and YHVH's displeasure.

To make the scenario more conclusive on the hopelessness of any ambition the custodians of darkness may harbor, not only are they under equipped, under-funded, under-supported etc., but every move the "enemy" makes, he needs to get permission to execute.

The reality of YHVH being the Source of all existence means that if YHVH is somehow removed from YHVH's unique position as Lucifer had intended (intends) to do, all existence would cease to be. Picture if you will, a tree with many branches and lush green leaves. The many branches are supplied their very existence by the roots of the tree. Consider now the few branches on the far side of the tree; just a handful of them with the ambition to uproot the tree. The intention is to cause all the branches to become brown and withered however the nourishment that causes the rest of the branches to be lush and green does not come from the brown and withered branches but rather from the root of the tree.

In a blind fury, the withered branches seek to take out the roots of the tree, not considering that if the root is taken out the entire tree would cease to exist; stem and branch; lush and withered, it would all cease to be.

Creation is sustained by the existence of YHVH because YHVH is existence.

Hebrews 1:3 Who being the brightness of *his* glory, and the express image of his person, and upholding all things by the word of his power, when he had by himself purged our sins, sat down on the right hand of the Majesty on high;

The war in Heaven, using the analogy of the tree is simply the attempt of the withered branches to continue to remain a part of the tree, when the root has decided it's time for those branches to be cut off and cast into the fire. Lucifer and his supporters are simply fighting for their lives using the minimal resources available to them as YHVH has restricted the flow of His Presence and Power to them.

# I AM EXISTENCE

And death and hell were cast into the lake of fire. This is the second death.  And whosoever was not found written in the book of life was cast into the lake of fire.

Revelations 20:14-15

# 8

# The Deck is Stacked

Lucifer's goose is cooked![3]

The chaos that is apparent in the earth and the consistent moral decline which makes it look as though darkness is prevailing, is simply the result of Satan's (Lucifer's) ability to convince men (humans) to smear themselves and one another with things that displease YHVH. When YHVH's displeasure is invoked, Satan has the authority to then bring such people, communities and nations into further bondage. In their bondage they look for relief which he (Satan/Lucifer) offers to them through some act or

---

[3] Colloquial phrase used in North America to indicate that the activities or plans of the person being discussed are doomed to fail.

rite which will further invoke the displeasure of YHVH and the cycle continues. Each time a person or community accepts or receives that which displeases YHVH into their lives, either actively or passively through ignorance or negligence, the noose is tightened a bit more.

Satan's grip on YHVH's creation only extends to the creatures under Adam's authority, up to and including Adam's descendants. YHVH had given Adam a term lease to exercise his authority over a certain aspect of creation, Adam handed over the authority to a usurper who has since gone on to ensure he infuses his corrupt nature into everything under the sphere of his authority.

The great news is; that sphere is *extremely* limited. The extent of YHVH's creation goes far beyond the bounds of what our minds can fathom. A large portion of that is wholly unaffected by Lucifer's corruption.

*YHVH made all things for His Pleasure. Only a small section of what He made is giving Him displeasure and suffering the consequences of His displeasure; an atmosphere in which Satan thrives, but YHVH does not like to dwell on His displeasure and is anxious to correct that malady just as a person would be anxious to take a stone out of his shoe.*

The thing keeping YHVH from rectifying this problem is the fact that all humanity, who YHVH was willing to make the ultimate sacrifice for, has not yet received the news that their continual dwelling in YHVH's displeasure is no longer necessary:

John 3:16  For God so loved the world, that he gave his only begotten Son, that whosoever believeth in him should not perish, but have everlasting life.

Perishing is a consequence of YHVH's displeasure, and everlasting life is a consequence of YHVH's Pleasure. When YHVH curbs the encroachment of YHVH's displeasure into YHVH's creation, what then happens to the ambassador/ embodiment of displeasure; the one who through his transgression became the first creature to invoke YHVH's displeasure and thus became the custodian of it for a predetermined period?

Psalms 73:27  For, lo, *they that are far from thee shall perish*: thou hast destroyed all them that go a whoring from thee.

I AM EXISTENCE

Who only hath immortality, dwelling in the light which no man can approach unto; whom no man hath seen, nor can see: to whom *be* honour and power everlasting. Amen.

I Timothy 6:16

# 9

# The Holiness of YHVH

Throughout the Bible and unto modern day, we see one peculiar characteristic of kings; they do not want anything that displeases them in their presence. This trait, that flawed humans occupying the position of royalty all exhibit is from of the refracted light of YHVH's Holiness.

In Nehemiah 2, Nehemiah recalls being fearful for his life because he didn't have a cheerful countenance as he served the king his beer.

Nehemiah 2:1-2  And it came to pass in the month Nisan, in the twentieth year of Artaxerxes the king, *that* wine *was* before him:

and I took up the wine, and gave *it* unto the king. Now I had not been *beforetime* sad in his presence. Wherefore the king said unto me, Why *is* thy countenance sad, seeing thou *art* not sick? this *is* nothing *else* but sorrow of heart. Then I was very sore afraid,

## When Queen Vashti displeased the king in Esther 1, she was no longer allowed into his presence till she died;

Esther 1:15 - 19   What shall we do unto the queen Vashti according to law, because she hath not performed the commandment of the king Ahasuerus by the chamberlains?
And Memucan answered before the king and the princes, Vashti the queen hath not done wrong to the king only, but also to all the princes, and to all the people that *are* in all the provinces of the king Ahasuerus.
For *this* deed of the queen shall come abroad unto all women, so that they shall despise their husbands in their eyes, when it shall be reported, The king Ahasuerus commanded Vashti the queen to be brought in before him, but she came not.
*Likewise* shall the ladies of Persia and Media say this day unto all the king's princes, which have heard of the deed of the queen. Thus *shall there arise* too much contempt and wrath.
If it please the king, let there go a royal commandment from him, and let it be written among the laws of the Persians and the Medes, that it be not altered, That Vashti come no more before king Ahasuerus; and let the king give her royal estate unto another that is better than she.

When Michal displeased King David, she was recorded as never having children after that. The children who had been entrusted into her care were eventually offered up to appease the Gibeonites;

2 Samuel 6:20 - 23  Then David returned to bless his household. And Michal the daughter of Saul came out to meet David, and said, How glorious was the king of Israel to day, who uncovered himself to day in the eyes of the handmaids of his servants, as one of the vain fellows shamelessly uncovereth himself!

And David said unto Michal, *It was* before the LORD, which chose me before thy father, and before all his house, to appoint me ruler over the people of the LORD, over Israel: therefore will I play before the LORD.

And I will yet be more vile than thus, and will be base in mine own sight: and of the maidservants which thou hast spoken of, of them shall I be had in honour.

Therefore Michal the daughter of Saul had no child unto the day of her death.

2 Samuel 21:1 -8  Then there was a famine in the days of David three years, year after year; and David enquired of the LORD. And the LORD answered, *It is* for Saul, and for *his* bloody house, because he slew the Gibeonites.

And the king called the Gibeonites, and said unto them; (now the Gibeonites *were* not of the children of Israel, but of the remnant of the Amorites; and the children of Israel had sworn unto them: and Saul sought to slay them in his zeal to the children of Israel and Judah.)

Wherefore David said unto the Gibeonites, What shall I do for you? and wherewith shall I make the atonement, that ye may bless the inheritance of the LORD?

And the Gibeonites said unto him, We will have no silver nor gold of Saul, nor of his house; neither for us shalt thou kill any man in Israel. And he said, What ye shall say, *that* will I do for you.

And they answered the king, The man that consumed us, and that devised against us *that* we should be destroyed from remaining in any of the coasts of Israel,

Let seven men of his sons be delivered unto us, and we will hang them up unto the LORD in Gibeah of Saul, *whom* the LORD did choose. And the king said, I will give *them.*

But the king spared Mephibosheth, the son of Jonathan the son of Saul, because of the LORD'S oath that *was* between them, between David and Jonathan the son of Saul.

But the king took the two sons of Rizpah the daughter of Aiah, whom she bare unto Saul, Armoni and Mephibosheth; and the five sons of Michal the daughter of Saul, whom she brought up for Adriel the son of Barzillai the Meholathite:

When Joseph was mourning the death of his father in sackcloth, he had to request the elders of Egypt to ask Pharaoh's permission to go bury his father. He could not enter Pharaoh's presence with sadness or mourning;

Genesis 50:4  And when the days of his mourning were past, Joseph spake unto the house of Pharaoh, saying, If now I have found grace in your eyes, speak, I pray you, in the ears of Pharaoh, saying,

Daniel and Esther were selected from among the best in the land to stand before their respective kings, yet they had to undergo extended periods of training and purification before they could even come into the kings presence for the first time. Daniel went through three and a half years of special diet and rigorous education, while Esther went through a full year of purification with perfumed oils, skin tenderizers and other such treatments.

One may dismiss all these as the abuse of power of perverted kings, but every perversion is a distortion of a genuine principle or legitimate Truth.

1 Timothy 6:15-16 Which in his times he shall shew, *who is* the blessed and only Potentate, the King of kings, and Lord of lords; Who only hath immortality, *dwelling in the light which no man can approach unto*; whom no man hath seen, nor can see: to whom *be* honour and power everlasting. Amen.

YHVH is Holy. We may not fully grasp what that means because some of us grew up understanding holiness to be the absence of cuss words from our lips and the ability to outwardly restrain our sexual urges. Holiness is far more than that.

One of the expressions of YHVH's Holiness is a mighty fiery purity that not only is unable to be corrupted but its raging fieriness eats up anything that is even a stitch lower in purity than it. As Moses' serpent swallowed up the serpents of the enchanters, so YHVH's Holiness consumes anything that doesn't measure up to it; and nothing measures up to it, nothing even comes close - even in Heaven.

I believe Lucifer, as 'the anointed cherub that covered' had to be made of special material; and the Bible does talk about the complexity and intricacy of his composition in Ezekiel 28. But even in spite of all the special material with which he was created to be able to refract YHVH's Light through precious stones for the rest of YHVH's creation to get a glimpse of YHVH's Holiness, Lucifer still had to stay far away from the actual Presence. It can be compared to a perimeter fence around a house with abundant grounds, so that the fence is far from the actual house. Imagine a regular sized log cabin sitting on twenty acres of land with a fence around the property. Even in his (Lucifer's) exalted position, he still had to give the Holiness of YHVH a wide berth.

When YHVH came to the earth as a man and became Yahshua (Jesus), He shed His Blood and that Blood became the covering (perimeter fence), but this time, it allows those who approach it to walk right up to the front door (of the log cabin). Only the Blood of YHVH could keep the fiery Holiness of YHVH from destroying those who come in His Name and through His Blood.

Halleluyah!

www.ingramcontent.com/pod-product-compliance
Lightning Source LLC
Chambersburg PA
CBHW070812170726
48000CB00017B/846